WOODBRIDGE AND ITS ENVIRONS

A selection of old photographs, paintings and memorabilia
arranged by Robert Blake and Lance Cooper

Foreword

With the passage of years the past becomes more interesting. When we are young we think little about days that have gone before. The years go by and with the death of grandparents and older generations, suddenly there is no one to ask. There remains however pictorial records of how places looked and how people dressed.

Before the middle of the nineteenth century illustrative information of the past was only obtainable from paintings and sketches. The invention of photography made available more accurate records of scenes from days gone by, beyond the ken of anyone living today. There are also more recent photographs taken in the lifetime of the present generation which recall the memories of the past for those people too young to remember what places looked like before modern reconstruction. They are very revealing.

Robert Blake and Lance Cooper have put together a collection of photographs, memoriabilia and paintings that will give much pleasure to both young and old. The past will come alive and stir emotions in many people. This book is an ideal medium for those who are interested in Woodbridge both past and present.

Daly Briscoe

A. Daly Briscoe

Seckford Lodge
Woodbridge

Acknowledgements

Our grateful thanks to the many who have contributed over the years with compiling this collection and have helped with its presentation.

Author's biographical sketch

The Blake family have lived in Suffolk for many generations and traded at Dallinghoo, some five miles from Woodbridge, for over a hundred years as wheelwrights, blacksmiths, undertakers and machinists. For more than twenty years Robert Blake was an antique dealer, having shops both at Melton and Saxmundham. During this time he assembled a large collection of illustrated material with local associations. From 1982 his career became more academic and he studied both at Oxford and the University of York, gaining an Honours Degree and University Diploma. Currently he is carrying out research and reading for a Doctorate.

Frank Blake, Robert's paternal grandfather, was a keen amateur photographer from the 1890s to the First World War, and the calibre of his work can be assessed by the examples illustrated in this book.

The collection of old photographs that Lance Cooper has amassed over 30 years began with a few 10 x 8 glass negatives taken by John Fosdyke.

Many people have contributed, as time progressed, to make a now considerable selection. With Robert Blake's keen interest Lance felt that now was the time for people to share our enthusiasm for early Woodbridge.

Introduction

Many would endorse the description of Woodbridge as "the most attractive small town in Suffolk".

In no way should Woodbridge be considered as a museum piece, situated in a time warp. It remains a vibrant and busy commercial and residential centre, serving particularly the Deben peninsula and its hinterland.

Four arteries can be identified which help to explain Woodbridge's rise and continuance as a thriving town. The Deben remains a wonderful backdrop, as illustrated by many of the photographs in this volume. However, in earlier times it was a busy commercial highway, particularly for heavy goods, exporting timber, cattle, grain and wool, and importing manufactured goods and raw materials (hence Barnes's large warehouse on the quay). Wilford Bridge, less than a mile upstream from Woodbridge, not only marks the lowest bridging point of the Deben but also its normal tidal limit. In earlier times, however, as this area was subject to periodic flooding, the present siting of Woodbridge was a natural choice for the development of wharfs and quays and offered protection for the hinterland, both for the town and its shipping, from northerly and westerly winds. Later, much trade came as a result of the London to Yarmouth turnpike passing through the town; this followed the route from Martlesham over the wooden bridge (Drybridge Hill) to the Bull, the town's main coaching inn, and from there northwards, passing through Melton and Ufford to Wickham Market. The advent of the railway initiated another major advance for the development of Woodbridge and its environs. After delays, it was eventually opened in 1859, when Thomas Churchyard, the local artist, was on the initial journey (the train overshot the platform at Woodbridge and therefore T.C. and his daughter were obliged to travel on to Melton Station, where they were charged three farthings each for the extra journey!). However, the railway line meant cheaper and easier transport, both for passengers and goods locally and nationwide, and further assisted in the decline of the Deben and the coach road. In the twentieth century the A12 now by-passes Woodbridge town and nearby villages, thus saving them from the worst effects of present-day road transport. Overall, it has resulted in the whole area becoming much more accessible, new businesses have appeared (and some traditional trades have been lost), housing has expanded, particularly in the last two decades, and tourism is now a major industry.

In any small town the importance of local characters cannot be underestimated. Woodbridge has its famous "wits" (Fitzgerald, Barton and Churchyard), but many lesser characters have endeared themselves throughout its history, and some of these appear in the following pages.

We have broadened the scope of this book to include the neighbouring villages of Martlesham, Melton and Ufford — they were closely associated with the main transport arteries, but they were until well into the twentieth century virtually self-contained and self-sufficient communities, only looking to Woodbridge for specialist services.

The aim of this volume is not simply to portray life from the past but also to show changes over the years and to compare and contrast some "vantage points" with how they are today. We have from necessity been selective; we hope in the future to produce further volumes which can be more specialist and enable us to illustrate different aspects of life in this area over the years.

These illustrations are laid out to help those enthusiasts who may like to contrast and compare the present day views with those of the past. Commencing at Martlesham through Woodbridge town to Melton and Ufford. There are maps on the inside front and back covers to assist you on your journey.

We hope you will share some of the fun and enjoyment we have experienced in preparing the following pages.

Martlesham Hill en route for Woodbridge

The 19th century Woodbridge murderer, ''Stumpy'' Brown, whose first victim was found under Martlesham Bridge.

The bridge and ford at Martlesham, 1926

Pre-war view of Read's blacksmith and wheelwright shops at junction of Sandy Lane and old A12

Seckford Hall North Elevation before restoration circa 1900

South Elevation

Woodbridge Reporter and Wickham Market Gazette

No. 5065 [Established 1859] THURSDAY, DECEMBER 5th, 1946. [Registered at the General Post Office as a Newspaper] ONE PENNY

JOTTINGS HERE & THERE

From the profits of the two nights' performances of the Connard Players' four one-act plays, the Oxford House St. John's Church Fund will benefit to the tune of £38 14s. which is a very creditable result to all concerned.

Two solos were rendered with feeling and confidence by Mrs. Baber (soprano) of Melton, at the Woodbridge Methodist Church on Sunday evening. The first was "The Holy City" (Stephen Adams) and secondly "Beside Still Waters" (Bernard Hamblen).

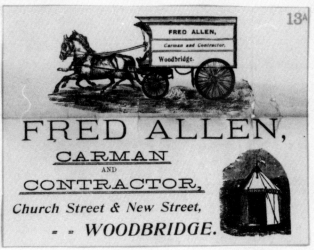

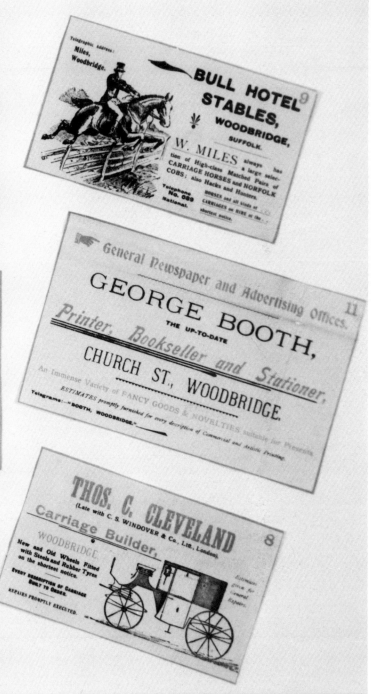

Selection of early 20th century Woodbridge businesses

13

19th century view of Woodbridge from Sutton

Walking on ice at Woodbridge Dock 1885

Bass's dock

Sid Desborough, the last miller at Haywards Mill

Four shots of exterior and interior of Hayward's mill

From the River Wall

As seen in the 1880s

Yacht launching at Everson's boatyard

Woodbridge Station (G.E.R.)

H.G. Cox, coal merchant

Gipsy encampment at the back of the Boat Inn

'Spanker' (Arthur Austin)

Woodbridge Scouts football team 1913–14

Towards Kingston Farm in the early 1930s

1905 Woodbridge Fire Brigade at their Cumberland Street Depot

Junction of Station Road and Cumberland Street

32   Watsham and Wilding Garage 1919

Towards the Cross Corner 1964

Post Office, Cross Corner, 1906

1911 Celebrations

Church Street at the turn of the century

Alfred Barnes' Emporium as it was in 1885 (destroyed by fire some 25 years later)

Quay Street in the early 1930s

PIONEERS of PURE SWEETS FOR THE PEOPLE.

A.S.KELL.

LYONS TEA

THE HOME MADE SWEET SHOP. IS WHERE YOU CAN PURCHASE PURE HOME-MADE SWEETS MANUF-CTURED FROM REFINED SUGARS ONLY. AND ABSOLUTELY FREE FROM ANY INJURIOUS INGREDIENTS

OIL PAINTI

POST CARDS.

Candy Bananas 20/-

A.S. Kell, local artist and pioneer of "pure sweets for the people" outside his Quay Street shop

Church Street: Davy Crowe's famed grocers; Sarah Meysey Thompson continues a long tradition

Miss Lilian Redstone in the Seckford Library

Mr. William Everett (on right) and his assistants

For King and Country, 1911

44   Market Hill

On market day

Sketch by Ann Churchyard

St Mary's Church at the turn of the century

View from St Mary's Church tower towards Sutton Hoo

Woodbridge Horse Show on Fen Meadow

Seckford Hospital in the 1890s

Woodbridge windmills as recorded by Thomas Churchyard 51

Tricker's Mill (unknown artist)

Buttram's Mill: Note miller on sails

Old and new Grammar School

54   Theatre Street: ''House of Correction'', complete with barred windows!

Market Hill 1888

Miss Turner outside her shop

An expanding business

Bell Inn, New Street — lower
part of building occupied
by Ipswich Tan Works
and Marine Stores

New Street School 1928

1911 Float

The proprietor ''awaiting business'' at 10 New Street

Now occupied by butcher and baker

Air-raid damage, August 12, 1915 — corner of Castle Street

Army vehicle (and mascot) after 1915 air-raid

Old Castle Street and St. John's Spire

St John's Church

On-going developments as recorded in the Thorofare

R.H. Rowland's pre-war workshop

R.H. Rowland and Son, 1947 (site of Woolworths)

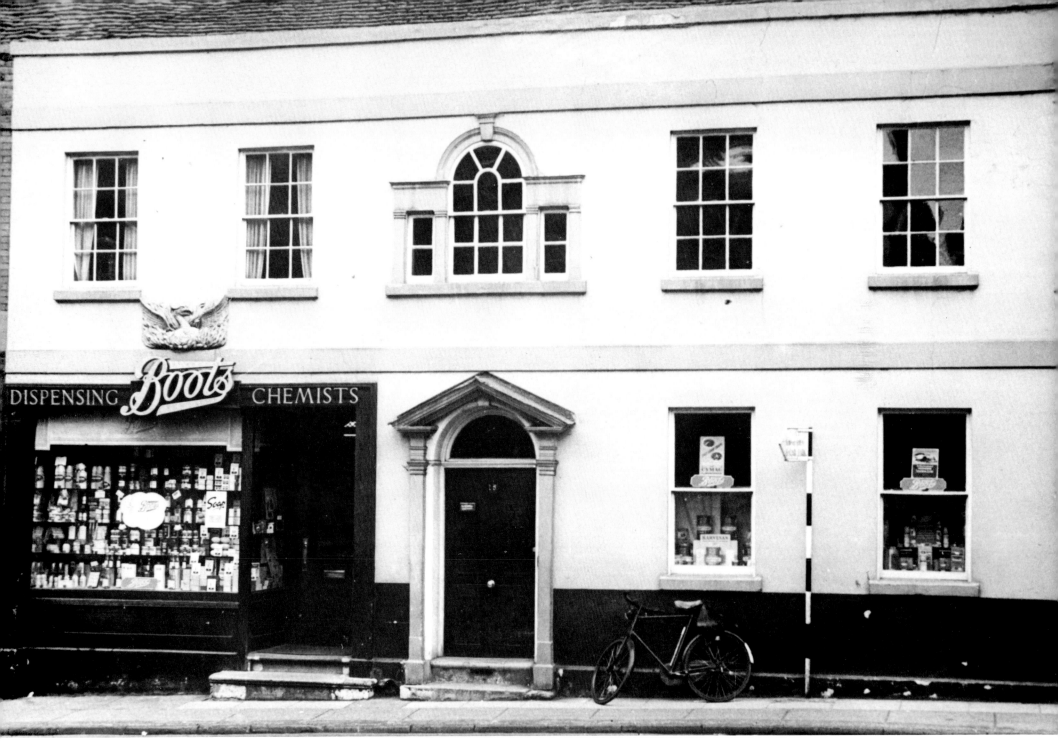

Boots, The Chemists

Royal Oak yard looking across Thorofare to H. Welton, Photographer

Centre Thorofare

Now occupied by Messrs Savages

Nunn's, now Victoria Wines and Sketchley's Cleaners

Milestone before being moved

Shelton Jewellers, later Walter Needs, Photographer, and now site of launderette and Midland Bank   77

Miss Cullingford at 43 Thorofare

Mr. Loder

Now site of Social Services Department

Thorofare looking north

Towards Melton Hill at turn of century

1920 A similar view 20 years later

Major Hart and Mrs. Hart at their home on Melton Hill

84

At Stephenson's Monumental Masons, 95 Thorofare, 1905

Miss Betty Hart

Woodbridge Postmaster at Pytches Road junction in 1905

Melton Hill, 1918

Fairhead and Sawyer, Melton

and with later modernisation

Mr. Daines (and Assistant)
standing outside his Melton works

1907 Melton Docks

Old gaol, Melton Street, 1929

"A prized acquisition"

1861 removal of Methodist Chapel due to "Ancient Light Laws"

Melton new Church upon completion, 1868

Wilford Old Bridge

Red House, Ufford

Ufford Board School

St Mary's, Lower Ufford, 1900

The Post Office and proprietor, Robert Cooper

1910: Interior of Ufford Place

Ufford Hill

Upper reaches of the Deben

Index